Make It Country

by
Judy Condon

Library of Congress Cataloging-in-Publications Data
Make It Country by Judy Condon
ISBN 978-0-9847028-4-8

Oceanic Graphic Printing, Inc.
105 Main Street
Hackensack, NJ 07601

Printed in China

Layout and Design by Pat Lucas,
    lucasketch_design@yahoo.com
Edited by Trent Michaels

Table of Contents

About the Author

Judy Condon is a native New Englander, which is evident in her decorating style and the type of antiques she collects and sells. Her real passion is 19thC authentic dry red or blue painted pieces. While Judy enjoyed a professional career as a teacher, Principal, and Superintendent of Schools in Connecticut, Judy's weekends were spent at her antique shop, *Marsh Homestead Country Antiques*, located in Litchfield, Connecticut.

When her husband, Jeff, was relocated to Virginia, Judy accepted an early retirement from education and concentrated her energy and passion for antiques into a fulltime business. Judy maintains a website, *www.marshhomesteadantiques. com* and has been a Power Seller on eBay® for 13 years under the name "superct".

Judy and her husband Jeff recently returned to their roots in New England and have completed renovating a 19thC cape in Massachusetts. The house was featured in her early 2012 book *Back Home – Simply Country* which included many before and after pictures. Judy has five children and five grandchildren and enjoys reading, golf, bridge, tennis, and volunteering in the educational system in St. Maarten. Judy does her best to provide teaching materials and children's books to the schools in St. Maarten with the hope of helping establish classroom libraries.

Judy's first 22 books in the "simply country" series, *Country on a Shoestring, Of Hearth and Home – Simply Country, A Simpler Time, Country Decorating for All Seasons, As Time Goes By, Country at Heart, Welcome Home – Simply Country, Home Again – Simply Country, The Warmth of Home, The Country Home, Simple Greens – Simply Country, The Country Life, Simply Country Gardens, The Spirit of Country, The Joy of Country, Holidays at a Country Home, A Touch of Country, Back Home – Simply Country, Just Country Gardens, The Place We Call Home, Autumn Harvest – Simply Country* and *Stockings Were Hung* have been instant hits and some are in their second printing. Judy continues to pursue additional homes and gardens and is working on four books for publication in 2013. Her books are available on her Website at *www.marshhomesteadantiques.com*, from *Amazon.com*, through her email *marshhomestead@comcast.net*, or by phone at 877-381-6682.

Introduction

Another holiday season is now part of the past. Kids are back in school, the special china for the holiday meal is back in the cupboards and we've started our diets and exercise program – after all it's a new year. While I'm left with wonderful memories, the decorations have been packed away for another year and I'm looking at a house which is WAY too bare for us country decorators! Spaces, only minutes ago filled with greens and berries, show bare wood. The center of the large farm table, for almost six weeks decorated with a bowl of vintage ornaments, now stands empty. The corner where the tree stood, or in my case, the corner in a number of rooms where a tree stood yesterday, is now desolate.

A new year – a new beginning! A fresh palette! What irony that retail stores have huge sales in January on home furnishings, paint, carpeting and all those accessories we need to re-create! I often use the winter months to rearrange the furniture or change the color of the trim in a room. Ah – what a can of paint can do! I love to paint. I find the change refreshing and the gratification instant. The fact that the cost is minimal is an extra plus. It has taken me three different colors to achieve the look I wanted in the guestroom and two different colors in the first floor bathroom before being satisfied with the outcome.

In *Make It Country*, you'll see the ingenuity of homeowners who have taken advantage of a fresh palette and brush to add warmth and enhance the country décor in their homes. Tracy Dodge and Steve Lipman applied a coat of black paint to a bed purchased at a local thrift shop and found the new bed blended beautifully with the antiques in their master bedroom. Sue and Joe Frank added life and color to their kitchen when they commissioned two antique collectors to stencil their kitchen floor for them. Gay and Craig Schneeman used subtle tones in the guestrooms of their B&B then used fabrics for accents. Sue Hveem and Nancy Lindberg utilize the same color on the trim throughout their homes allowing the subtle color to add, rather than detract, from the simple placement of antiques and folk art. Christa and Billy Balderson are in a category of their own as they use paint to transform all their pieces of furniture and have even invented a process for aging. The Eakins used paint wherever possible in their home, converted from a granary, to add color and lighten the room, while the Mariano's used a variety of paint colors to blend the original structure with the addition to their large Pennsylvania home. Sandy Worley pulls colors from her patterned rugs for the paint color on her trim; drawing the eye upward and tying the room together.

There's still time! Go for it! As you've heard me ask before, "What will it cost me to fix it if I don't like the outcome?" Grab a brush – Make It Country!

Chapter 1

Gay and Craig Schneeman

Gay and Craig Schneeman are both natives of New Jersey and have known each other since they were nine years old. Craig's sister was Gay's best friend and childhood playmate. While they each almost married someone else at one point, they reconnected and have been married over 40 years. Craig taught school when they were first married but elected to leave the profession and pursue his passion as a carpenter . . . following in the footsteps of his father and grandfather. Gay is Director of Medical Imaging for Kennedy University Hospital in southern New Jersey, but both find the time to operate a successful bed & breakfast at their Mannington, New Jersey home.

The brick section of their home was built circa 1735 and the wood addition at the back added in 1991. The house was originally a large Quaker farm. By today's standards the house would not be thought of as large but in the early 18thC it would have been considered a mansion. Research shows that the house was built by the Barrett family, thus the name of Craig and Gay's B&B – Barrett Plantation House. The home is located in Salem County, an area rich in American Revolution history. Gay has completed extensive research and discovered that their home played a significant role

during the Revolution. In 1778, when Washington's starving army camped at Valley Forge, a group of soldiers from Salem County knew where the farmers were hiding their cattle and grain. A soldier by the name of Anthony Wayne was ordered by General Washington to take a group of soldiers, return to Salem County, and bring supplies back to Valley Forge. Wayne and his men rounded up 150 head of cattle which they drove out King's Highway and camped on the grounds of Craig and Gay's home prior to their return through Trenton and back across the river to Valley Forge.

When Gay and Craig first took possession of the house, they immediately made cosmetic changes and Craig remodeled the kitchen area. He replaced the vinyl floors with tile and the Formica counters with cherry.

Gay painted the cabinetry and the trim throughout most of the house with a beige she had seen in a magazine from the Martin Senour company, which was contracted to make repro paint for Colonial Williamsburg.

Craig made the tall clock in the corner as a gift to his mother on her 80th birthday. He also made the farm table which holds a decoy carved by a local carver, Jode Hillman.

The tile backsplash covers white ceramic tile and was intended as a temporary fix until Gay decided what she wanted to use. The tile backsplash, purchased at Home Depot, are actually plastic sheets. Gay reports they are easy to clean, the pewter color is perfect, and she is happy with the look.

The island surface is Corian. The bow back Windsor chairs are new pieces.

A massive granite farm sink weighing 300 lbs is located beneath the window which looks out onto the herb and cutting gardens.

Craig built the cupboard to hold some of Gay's stoneware collection. The large spongeware piece on the left side was Craig's grandmother's potato salad bowl.

Craig built the cupboard with a special space to accommodate the large spongeware cooler.

Two tin-lidded large apothecary jars stand on top of a narrow jelly cupboard that Craig made to fit in the hallway leading to the room where they spend most of their time.

This room contained the 19thC kitchen; Gay surmises there might have been a summer kitchen when the house was first built. The cabinet houses the television, and while Gay and Craig recognize that the L hinges are not period, they like the contrast with the Daphne Room's beige paint. The gun

is a fowling piece made by the Ketland Co. of Birmingham, England, founded in 1760. The company began trading overseas in 1790 and ceased in 1831. The guns were made in England and shipped to the USA in parts, where a local gunsmith assembled the gun. The term, "lock, stock, and barrel" originated from these fowling pieces. A shot flask also hangs from the fireplace.

Another decoy carved by Jode Hillman stands on the mantel between pairs of Williamsburg blue and white mugs.

Gay and Craig use the fireplace occasionally for cooking, particularly when their two grandsons visit, as they are fascinated by the process.

An early gameboard holds a collection of iron cooking utensils. The picture of a skewer with heart cutout picks up the rich tones and hand-hewn marks of the fireplace lintel.

Craig and Gay have not been able to determine what the framed opening, now sealed off, was used for; they speculate a window but now use it to create a vignette.

The large corner cupboard was purchased at Royal Port Antiques in Salem County; the natural pine surface creates a striking contrast to the cupboard's interior paint. The two small chairs on the third shelf down were irresistible; while shopping at **RW Burnham Antiques** in Ipswich, Massachusetts, Gay and Craig discovered that Craig is a Burnham descendant. The chairs flank a stoneware batter pitcher – Gay's favorite piece in the cupboard.

Both the contemporary wall shelf and spoon rack were purchased at a now closed local New Jersey shop.

Gay decorated the parlor, which also serves as a dining and sitting area for guests, in soothing tones of navy and beige. Craig fashioned the corner cupboard which stands beside a reproduction Habersham Plantation clock. Beside the wing back chair, a small table with Queen Anne legs and birds eye maple top was made by Craig.

The cherry drop leaf table is early and purported to be a Rhode Island piece. A Canton ginger jar is filled with fresh flowers from Gay's cutting garden.

A 1764 map showing the house and the Barrett family property hangs on the wall above a bucket bench. Craig and Gay have decided to collect only Remy stoneware pieces. R.C. Remy is a famous local potter and Craig and Gay feel fortunate to have found a few of his pieces; the crock on the bottom shelf to the left features Remy's hallmark.

A friend of Craig's asked him to hold the ship model his father had made. The ship has now been in their possession for four years and their friend has determined it looks too good on their cabinet to take it back. Gay has created a naval vignette using two pieces of scrimshaw and a contemporary deck prism. The prism's flat surface would be fixed to the ship's main deck while its point directed sunlight to areas below.

Three Canton ginger and storage jars are displayed on the mantel. The portrait, signed by Moses Billings, is an oil on canvas of Sarah McCarthy of Erie, Pennsylvania. The contemporary cherry tea table holds a Williamsburg tea set.

While Gay and her daughters were cleaning out the home of an aunt who had died, each daughter asked for the small chest. To settle the argument, Gay took the piece herself which was painted with thick white paint. After she had it dry-scraped, Gay was pleasantly surprised by the outcome – a Federal style chest with inlaid ovals. The slender hanging wall shelf is filled with early Canton pieces. The little table behind the wing back holds one of many Canton ginger jar lamps Gay owns.

Gay and Craig Schneeman 13

The cherry circa 1830 drop leaf table was purchased at The Yellow Garage in Mullica Hill, New Jersey. On top, a small pine two-drawer chest stands below a Chippendale Federal style mirror.

A tri-corn hat and Canton lamp are displayed on the country Sheridan chest in the front hallway. The oil portrait features a wealthy Quaker lady – so determined by her dress.

In the hallway leading to the back room from the front entrance, a framed flag with 42 stars belonging to Craig's family holds a spot on the wall above a Federal drop leaf table belonging to Gay's family. A 19thC fire bucket can be seen hanging at the edge of the picture.

I wanted to include the small watercolor because of its vibrant color and three-dimensional effect; it was done by Sharon Trenoweth, a New England folk artist.

The study to the right of the front entrance is finished with beautiful pine panels. The portrait above the mantel is of Samuel McCarthy, husband of Sarah, whose portrait was seen in the parlor. Two Staffordshire dogs stand on the mantel. On the table at the edge of the picture an early green onion bottle is barely visible.

The drop leaf table was found at The Yellow House Garage, while the ledger on top is from an old country store and holds entries from 1814-1835.

A matched set of Mason decoys, dating to 1900, belonged to Craig's grandfather. A rifle belonging to Craig's father hangs below them.

Craig and Gay call the decoy 'the hissing goose'. It stands on top of an early corner cupboard found in a Mullica Hill home.

The Dickinson Suite, so named after the Dickinson family who owned the property for many years, is painted in a pale, soft gray-green.

The fireplace is one of six in the house.

Gay and Craig named the suite seen above The Morris Suite after a former superintendent of schools in Salem County who owned the house for a time and completed some restoration.

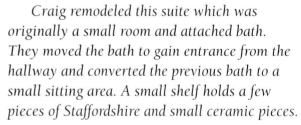

Craig remodeled this suite which was originally a small room and attached bath. They moved the bath to gain entrance from the hallway and converted the previous bath to a small sitting area. A small shelf holds a few pieces of Staffordshire and small ceramic pieces.

The grounds of the Schneeman's home are manicured. Craig built all the gates leading to both the kitchen garden and the herb and cutting gardens across the driveway.

A pebble path leads to the back through boxwood hedges. Craig totally remodeled the adorable country shed.

Gay has added wonderful country accents. Craig built the pergola in the side yard where guests can enjoy a quiet moment.

Barrett Plantation House B&B is open year round; there are two guest suites with private bathrooms available from $95-$120 per night depending on the season and include a cocktail hour and full gourmet breakfast. Each suite is equipped with many amenities including a hair dryer, central air conditioning, and WiFi.

Craig and Gay maintain a website www.Barrettsplantationhouse.com and may be reached by phone at 856-935-0812 or via email barrettsplantationhouse@comcast.net.

Gay and Craig Schneeman 19

Chapter 2

Pat and Gordon Eakin

One of the most unique homes I've photographed is that of Pat and Gordon Eakin of Lucinda, Pennsylvania. Pat and Gordon renovated a feed mill built in the early 1900's alongside an abandoned railroad track in a quiet part of this rural town. Town records are scarce; it appears that the mill was a cooperative effort by the townsfolk, one of whom donated the land. Pat and Gordon found the property six years ago and moved there from the Pittsburgh area. Gordon had just retired from the Department of Labor and Pat was ready to retire from the antique business they operated for 10 years after having run a bait and tackle store for 26 years. Their love of primitives, antiques, and collectibles made the mill the perfect home for them.

A sweeping porch on the side of the house is decorated with plants and antiques. Pat planted succulents in a display of early grain scoops. The shelf displays a variety of vintage chicken feeders. Pat filled a few of the cubbies with abandoned bird nests.

An old corn sheller retains its beautiful original blue paint. The rusty tin Shaker sign is early.

The main floor consists of one large room without interior walls or dividers. There are, however, 25 grain chutes that carried grain from the third floor for bagging; the chutes divide the room into segments ideal for various vignettes. The reader should imagine that he/she is walking in the front door from the porch and I will describe how each section is arranged around a large circle.

Pictured in front of the double door, a pendulum spinning wheel features an iron ball as a weight. The church pew retains its original pumpkin paint.

On the early painted bench, a wind-up tin toy resembles a carousel as the pieces spin. A hooked rug, crafted by Diane Denmead, is displayed with two samplers on either side of the window; wrought by sisters from New Hampshire, the samplers are dated 1804 and 1810.

Across the floor from the pew, one of the grain chutes is held together with bands. Gordon uses the bands to display a collection of advertising cards. The butter churn with dry blue paint was found in Massachusetts. A kerosene can in a red wooden frame rests on the floor. Suspended over the churn is a stack of old drug store receipts and prescriptions dating from 1942-1949, which have been preserved on the original metal stake. A scrub board featuring various sized holes is affixed to the brick. A paper parade top hat with a gauzelike ribbon stands atop the bread case which is filled with old candy tins and children's toys. The bread case is resting on a large store counter with six drawers that was purportedly part of a dress shop.

Pat and Gordon collect vintage marshmallow containers, one of which marked 'Edward Sugar Puff' is seen on the top of the store counter.

The glass case on the right side of the counter holds a display of Arrow collars. The lidded box in front is a Neatslene shoe grease box with several tins of polish. The advertising on front claims the polish "makes work shoes manure proof"!

The grain bagger was semi-automatic and quite sophisticated. The bag rested on the scale and was filled from the chute. When the bag reached its proper weight, the flow of grain stopped.

Looking at the front entrance area from the opposite side, the bench in front of the church pew peeks out from behind the wingchair. A vintage hooked bunny dressed in old-fashioned clothes and suede shoes can be seen at the edge of the picture. A horse feedbox holds magazines beside the chair.

Antique and new pewter from Olde World Pewter is displayed on the mantel beneath the print of Abraham Lincoln. An old reflector oven rests on the hearth.

Across from the mantel, a hutch table with red paint holds an early marked stack of Frye measures. The table rests against another bagger marked 'S. Howes Co, Silver Creek, New York'. A standing butter churn with dry mustard paint can be seen at the corner of the picture. The hanging octagonal light consists of 10 lanterns; it would have been used in a two-story store and suspended over the counter area.

On the opposite side, a small sitting area is arranged with the large canted chute on the back wall.

The chalkboard indicates all the items for sale.

A standing doughbox with dry paint holds a Chadwick's spool cabinet once used to store cotton threads.

A Schneeman lamp stands in the zinc-lined well of an early gray painted dry sink. On the floor is a vintage toy Turner fire truck.

A brass stencil is displayed on the front of a mustard chimney cupboard. The stencil would have been used to paint the top of a whiskey barrel by a local distiller. Old peanut butter cans are seen on top. Tucked in the corner is a small replica of the mill left to the Eakins by the previous owner. A small potty chair in blue paint rests on the floor beside the cupboard. A broom holder advertising Gold Medal flour stands between chutes.

In front of the window, a divided grain bin holds crafted wooden houses. On the side of the chute is an old cigar advertising sign.

As a visitor walks along the right side of the large room and toward the back, a beam is seen holding a nail display board with sizes and prices. In the back corner is a child's highchair which stands beside an old grain bin. Pat and Gordon use this area, which fills the back right corner of the room, for dining.

The large chalkboard over the scale was shown in the sitting area, as well. A small field basket holds flowers on top of a small grain bin. The piece on the floor is an early wooden trencher.

A slant top desk rests on a 19thC standing dry sink with wonderful dry red paint. Above, at the top of the window, assorted Planter's peanut jars and pitchers are displayed. A 15-gallon crock is tucked under the sink beside a manganese crock and jug.

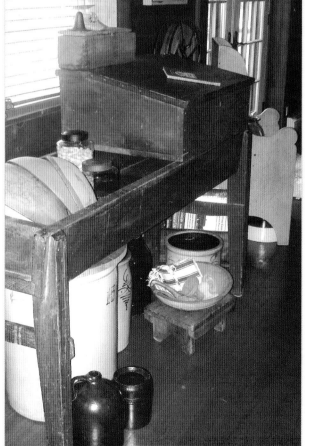

The piece in the corner is actually a butcher's meat case, which would have been displayed on the delivery wagon; it stands on end and has slanted lift-top doors so the butcher could reach the meat for sale. At the edge of the picture, a spoon rack with putty gray paint is filled with pewter spoons. An Ann Rea theorem hangs on the wall in the corner.

A Fairbanks scale is standing at the end of the dining area and holds an assortment of early shoes. Beside it, an early conductor's uniform is displayed on the form. The broom rack is early and holds an assortment of vintage brooms.

Walking across the back of the room from right to left, a visitor passes an old post office front. Vintage Reed's Butterscotch tins are stacked on top. An antique display case holds pieces crafted by Debbie Thibault; atop can be seen a grouping of miniature gauze American flags.

A large grain bin in gray paint stands beneath a two-drawer shelf with original red paint. A postcard holder stands at the end beneath an early postcard sign.

From back to front along the left side of the room, a large old auger is encased in a box which creates a shelf for two feathered barnyard animals.

The mustard Windsor chair is a new piece from the Warren Chair Company in Rhode Island.

A vintage top hat sits in the well of an old apple green dry sink.

A vintage parade costume is tucked under the stairs. Hanging over the rail is a vintage quilt, which, when held up to the light, black cotton seeds are revealed inside.

The stairs are lined with crocks depicting Biblical events. A display case which held nuts and bolts came out of an old hardware store. Behind it, a large blue grain bin consists of three sections. On top can be seen a claw foot platform scale.

The kitchen area at the back originally served as the mill's office. A five-board top scrub table is surrounded by early Windsors. The curtain at the back conceals a door to the deck. A collection of vintage tin containers is displayed on a shelf above the door and over the cabinet above the sink.

Deep recessed window sills allow room for a display of vintage tin pieces. The double-handled egg coddler holds two dozen eggs. Also seen are some early cookie cutters, a small kerosene light, and an ice cream measure on the right side.

In the corner, an old chestnut roaster hangs below a tin strainer. Two old egg crates are displayed on top of the cupboard. The trencher is filled with tinware and a collection of nutmeg graters.

The child's cradle with worn red paint was found in Connecticut.

To the left of the headboard, Pat has enclosed two old books in shadowbox frames.

Pat found the brass bed in the guestroom for $10. Coverlets from Family Heirloom Weavers in earth tones cover the bed.

A 19thC wagon box sits on top of the dry sink with green paint.

Pat calls the upholstered chair a "timeout" chair since naughty children can't see left or right when placed there for misbehaving!

Pat and Gordon expanded an outbuilding, part of the original property, and created a life-size replica of a general store. They have not only succeeded in preserving some of the local history but also satisfied their interest in collecting. They have opened their doors and currently offer tours to school children allowing them to learn first hand what life was like "in the old days". Last year they were fortunate to welcome some guests who remembered the mill and were able to share their recollections.

Chapter 3

❦ ※ ❧

Susan Hveem

In preparation for our move to Virginia in 2002, Jeff and I placed our 1764 Connecticut home on the market. Knowing that Sue and Harvey Hveem, frequent customers of my antique shop in Litchfield, were looking for an older home, I contacted them. Sue and Harvey visited and were interested but the house sold to another party before they could make an offer. I closed the shop when we moved to Virginia and lost contact with Sue and Harvey. I was pleased when their daughter contacted me. She thought I would be interested in featuring the 18thC house her mother lived in. Sue had followed my path through my books and was willing to open her lovely home.

Sue and her late husband, Harvey purchased the 1792 Woodbury, Connecticut, home in 2002. It is the sixth house they have remodeled and not the earliest, but clearly the favorite. Sue admits Harvey was the driving force behind the renovations and moves. Harvey was a 20-year retired Navy veteran while Sue managed the nearby Southbury Training School—but their real passion has always been antiques. They operated a business, *1734 Antiques*, and although they did not have a shop they exhibited at a number of country shows each year.

When I entered the house, I was immediately struck by the simplicity of the decorating, the open space, and warm colors. Sue said she always wanted to create a welcoming and

comfortable home and she certainly has. Sue used Benjamin Moore "Lenox Tan" on the trim throughout much of the house. The living room is a combination of old and new. The couch and the mustard chair were purchased at *The Seraph*, while the red chair came from *Angel House* in Brookfield, Massachusetts.

The painting is early and was found at an auction in New York State. Sue and Harvey found many of their pieces at auctions or thrift and consignment shops. The early chest in mustard paint with blue stencils is a Pennsylvania piece purchased locally in Connecticut. The wedding band hogscraper was a gift to Sue from Harvey. The shorebird is one of many the Hveems own; it was carved by Richard Morgan of Connecticut, a carver who used real eyes and old nails to create his birds.

The pewter chargers on the mantel are all early. The redware piece on the left is old and holds pieces of cane used to light candles. On the right is an early redware striker; it holds matches and features a striker on the side. The two Canton ginger jar lamps were found at a consignment shop.

The tall piece with early red paint is actually an early clock case. Sue displays a reproduction tin sconce on top. The oil painting shows a group of chickens and pigeons. Harvey had an extensive collection of pigeon figures and was also a pigeon flyer hobbyist. The painting was done by his daughter Monica LaRose as a gift, the second painting she had ever done.

A Greg Schooner redware lamp sits on an antique tiger maple table with stretcher base. Sue found the painting at a thrift shop; she and Harvey were pleasantly surprised with its appraised value.

A reproduction cabinet holds a television and, on top, an early New York State basket and a weathervane found in New Hampshire. The chairs on either side of the cupboard are early ladder backs found locally in Woodbury.

A stack of early painted boxes is tucked beside the door leading to the screened porch. The blue box from Pennsylvania is Sue's favorite – a gift from her son.

The porch is painted with Benjamin Moore "Shenandoah Taupe". Sue leaves the porch intact through the winter in case she is surprised with a warm day and has occasion to use it. The huge basket was found in Washington, Connecticut. Note the creative lamp on the table made using an early mortar.

Two early bow back Windsor chairs, found in New York, stand beside a small sawbuck table with early red wash base. The red hanging cupboard was purchased at Milltown Primitives in North Stonington, Connecticut; it holds two pieces of reproduction yellowware with the seaweed pattern purchased at East Knoll Pottery in Torrington, Connecticut.

Sue and Harvey found the dining room table and chairs at Brimfield, made by a craftsman from Lincoln, Maine. The two-drawer pine blanket chest dates to 1832. The four-drawer apothecary was found in New Hampshire; another Richard Morgan bird stands beside it. The painting depicts an Indian hiding behind a tree watching a deer.

The built-in corner cupboard holds collections of baskets and samplers, all rendered by their daughter, Monica. The interesting basket on the top shelf is a Shaker piece which Sue uses to carry pies.

Sue has a fondness for miniature baskets. One of her favorites is the black-handled basket seen below left; it was made by and purchased from Jonathan Klein.

Much to Harvey's dismay, Sue was determined to buy the oil painting depicting a pastoral scene of grazing sheep at a New York State auction that now hangs between the windows; Sue has never regretted spending what she did to own it. Sue found the blue and white vase on the table for $5 at a thrift shop.

An early apothecary jar holds a collection of clay marbles, while an early green onion bottle stands beside a blue and cream piece of pottery found at a tag sale. Both the painted document box and toleware box were purchased at a local antique shop.

The trim paint in the bedroom off the dining room is Old Village "Rittenhouse Ivory". The maple bed fits perfectly in the room, which has many openings and was not easy to decorate. Their daughter made the colorful patchwork quilt on the bed from scraps of upholstery, one of which matches the couch in the living room. The spread and pillow sham are from Family Heirloom Weavers. Sue commissioned a local artisan to make the hooked rug. The box hanging beside it was purchased at Toll House Antiques in Bantam, Connecticut. An early captain's brass candleholder and early blue painted dough bowl stand on a table, which was covered with thick white paint before Sue and Harvey stripped it down and oiled it.

The red hanging cupboard with glass front holds a wide variety of carved pigeons from all over the U.S., Germany, and England. Harvey's hunt for pigeons, according to Sue, was a great source of conversation in every shop and booth they entered.

I've already asked Sue to let me know when she is ready to part with the Pennsylvania bench in blue paint.

Sue wanted to keep the bathroom off the first floor bedroom simple. Their son-in-law, Gary LaRose, a cabinet maker from New York, built the cherry-top vanities which are painted with Old Village "Rittenhouse Ivory"; he also built the matching mirrors. The chair in the corner is early and stands beneath another sampler by their daughter Monica.

The far side of the dining room serves as a hallway to the kitchen. The drop leaf table in the hallway was found in pieces in a shop. A stack of early pantry boxes, a carved Richard Morgan bird, and a redware lamp that Harvey made stand on the table.

The pencil sketch on the wall shows one of the Hveem's earlier homes. The small table is called a Windsor seat table and was found at the Hartford Antique Show. The lamp is a new Greg Schooner piece.

The two-drawer William & Mary blanket chest with old English pulls and ball feet is tucked in the corner. Sue shared an interesting fact that she had just learned about the false drawer fronts of early blanket chests. According to her source, the amount of tax levied on owners depended on how many drawers their blanket chests had. Most chests were made with two real drawers; two false drawers were added to give the appearance of more without the higher tax. The ladder back arm chair was made by Hoffman & Woodward of Pennsylvania. The sampler over the chest is dated 1817; beneath it stands a burl bowl.

A built-in book shelf across the hallway from the blanket chest holds first edition books by Joseph C. Lincoln about Martha's Vineyard and Cape Cod. Assorted redware and pottery are displayed, as well. One of Sue's favorite pieces is a small chalkware squirrel standing on a small bench and located on the second shelf down, far left.

Sue traded the cant back cupboard with a friend and is the first to state, "I won!" It is a Spanish Brown 19thC piece which Sue has filled with old and new redware and mochaware; the new mochaware was made by Don Carpentier. The lollipop-handled box is old. The newer child's chair with splay legs was found at Brimfield and used by each of Sue and Harvey's grandchildren.

Sue refers to the room off the kitchen as the Gathering Room and says it is the most lived-in room in the house. The round hutch table was purchased at The Seraph. The chairs were made by Hoffman & Woodward. An early Regulator clock, made in Ansonia, Connecticut, hangs between the windows.

The corner cupboard was found locally; its blue interior creates a pretty visual with the seaweed pattern on the yellowware pieces. The small figures are chalkware turkeys.

The oil painting depicting a flock of chickens is early. The lift-top blanket chest holds a lidded yellowware crock and pantry box.

Another Richard Morgan bird stands on top of a stack of early narrow painted benches tucked behind a chair.

Sue painted the oak kitchen cabinets and added old knobs; Gary refashioned the base of the cabinets to look like old cupboards. The shelving was purchased at The Seraph. The counter tops are butcher block. Sue uses the early apothecary on the counter to hold spices. She loves to collect cutting boards and displays them with lots of new and old yellowware. The canister set is new and was purchased at East Knolls Pottery. A small shelf, shown left, holds a yellowware custard cup and bird. The shelf conceals a thermostat and was purchased from Newton Country Mill in Newton, Connecticut.

The early spoon holder in red paint was scraped down; remnants of layers of white paint are still visible.

Gary built the large cupboard which houses the microwave and dishware. The refrigerator is concealed in a pantry behind the back door. Sue and Harvey found the table with green base at The Elephant Trunk in New Milford, Connecticut – a huge outdoor flea market.

A small cutting board with tombstone top stands beside another cutting board dated 1812. Sue uses mineral oil on all her pieces, wipes each wooden piece in the house and lets it sit for 2-3 hours, and then wipes each down with a clean soft rag. The oil creates a nice shine to the patina and protects the wood at the same time from drying out.

The room seen right is son Billy's room when he comes to visit. Sue and Harvey were appalled that someone had painted the beams white but elected to leave them. The bedspread was purchased for $25 at Home Goods.

A six-board chest holds a small box and a basket of stuffed animals. The picture between the windows depicts a cat, a favorite animal of Billy's when he was a child. The mouse adds a whimsical touch!

The landing at the top of the stairs is large enough for Sue's office area. The arm chair is early. A black chest holds a wonderful, early basket from New York State.

The master bathroom upstairs is huge. In addition to the vanity, Sue was able to fit a cottage pine 19thC chest to store linens.

Sue and Harvey purchased the shelf beside it from the previous owners.

Sue found the four poster bed at a consignment shop and was able to just barely fit it into the master bedroom. The silhouettes present images of Sue and her four children. The blanket chest in early red wash at the foot of the bed holds a basket filled with dried hydrangeas from Sue's garden.

A cottage pine chest stands beside a Queen Anne chair. The walls are painted with a Benjamin Moore paint called "Pittsfield Buff".

The apothecary spice box was in pieces when found; Harvey was able to reassemble it and the box is now one of Sue's favorite pieces.

A tall two-door chimney cupboard with red wash holds a three-sided glass lantern. A reverse glass painted mirror hangs beside it. An antique dealer explained to Sue that the reason mirrors were painted on top was because taxes levied on homeowners were based on the size of their mirrors; the painting on top reduced the tax.

Chapter 4

Christa and Billy Balderson

Normally when I pull up in front of a home I'm going to photograph, I imagine what the inside might look like. When I drove to Billy and Christa Balderson's home in Crisfield, Maryland, I pictured a modest single-story home with traditional colonial furnishings. So much for my supposition! I was shocked when I stepped inside the front door.

Billy works in the asphalt business and is a much too modest, self-taught carpenter. According to Christa, she only has to describe or show Billy a picture of something and he makes it. Their home is 26 years old; they purchased it from Billy's parents in 1995. At the time, it was decorated with what Christa describes as "cutesy" country-lots of pink hearts and geese. Billy and Christa began by ripping out carpeting and removing wallpaper. Christa described herself then as a collector of colonial pieces, but found she wanted to go back in time.

Christa and Billy are now committed to first period decorating and have made or repurposed nearly every piece of furniture in their home. Christa relies on books, books, and more books; she gathers her ideas and uses her active imagination to create accents. With a son and two grandchildren, Christa admits she would much rather spend their money on the family than on decorating. As a result, it is hard to believe what Billy and Christa have created "on a shoestring".

While Billy and Christa love what they do and the result of their labors, their parents don't understand. Recently, Christa's mother, upon seeing a doll Christa had made, lovingly remarked, "I would have bought you a doll, honey. You didn't have to make anything that looks that bad." Billy's mother simply feels her son and his wife have created a home with "dirty rags" hanging everywhere!

The front door opens directly into the Keeping Room. Billy lined the walls and ceiling with boards. He also made the tall settle bench in the corner. Christa never pays more than $20 for a barrel and finds most of them at yard sales. The hanging drape, used as a divider, is a painter's cloth which Christa dyed and aged. Christa uses a variety of dyes and solutions to create variations in her textiles. She has used coffee, tea, or packaged dyes. Clumps of dried onions are seen atop one of the barrels.

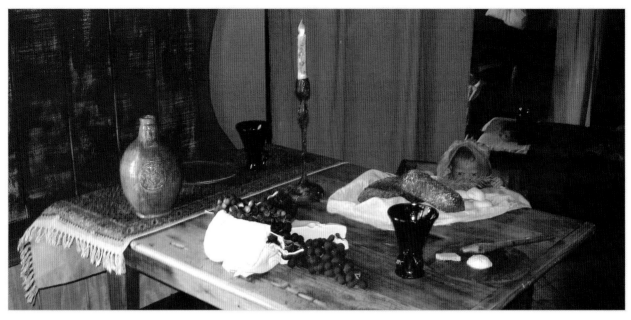

The table was purchased at The Country House in Salisbury, Maryland, and is a piece fashioned by a company named Knock on Wood. Artificial grapes, goblets, and an ovoid jug are displayed on top. The wedge of Swiss cheese and loaves of bread are real, dried on cheesecloth by Christa. Christa made the plum pudding wrapped in cheesecloth which hangs from a wooden dryer Billy created.

Christa made the broom from twigs and bamboo which grows freely in her son's backyard. Christa found the stool at the end of the table at Goodwill Industries for $5. Billy and Christa have developed a system to achieve the distressed appearance of their furniture. They first spray the piece with flat black paint and then either lightly sand or rub off some of the paint. While the piece is still wet, they brush on a solution of mineral spirits and roofing tar. Sometimes Christa also sprinkles on cinnamon before the piece has dried to create a rusty look.

Billy made the large peel and Christa made the hanging black shelf where she has placed a salt dough pie wrapped in cheesecloth.

Christa found the fireplace at a yard sale; Billy made the surround and mantel. Christa bought two of the treen chargers on the mantel at Pier I and aged them. The garland is made of dried sweet potatoes. Also seen on the mantel is an early iron Betty lamp base and bowl of flax. The hutch table, which holds authentic dried corn, was painted with thick white paint when they found it but their magic formula converted it into a piece which fits perfectly with their décor.

Christa found long seed pods in a friend's yard and has hung them to dry by the side of the mantel.

Christa made the corn husk broom leaning against the mantel while Billy created the hornbeam on the floor.

The small table in front of the fireplace is a plant stand which Christa painted; it holds a rusted griddle, purchased for $3, and real slabs of dried smoked bacon.

A large settle and sawbuck table, both made by Billy, stand in the area to the right of the mantel. Christa found the cape, which is not old, at Smoke and Fire. The wall paint is a Lowe's color the name of which Christa was unable to recall. Christa shared that, when trying to achieve the right

colors for painting or dying a piece, she uses crayons and paper and keeps blending colors until she is satisfied. The ladderback chairs began as unfinished pieces and have been transformed with Billy and Christa's aging process. The pumpkin is one of many Christa buys at Michael's retail store out of season at 50% off. She ages them and, in this case, hollowed out the base, punctured small holes in the sides, and uses it as a cheese safe over the wedge of cheese on the table.

The portrait of the early 18thC woman was an eBay® find, while the sconce was purchased at Goodwill Industries for $2. The pheasant at the end of the table was purchased from a taxidermist, while the candlestand was found for $15 at a consignment shop.

Christa had a difficult time finding the right cupboard for a corner in the Keeping Room until she found a bookcase at Walmart. She removed the shelves and painted the bookcase with the magic black solution to create the exact look she wanted. Christa found the Styrofoam gourds at Walmart which were originally a bright orange. She mixed folk art paints until she found the color she wanted, then painted thin lines with a brush and darker paint. The drying rack in front was made by Christa's son and was a gift to her.

Billy removed part of the wall leading to a small spare bedroom and created a bed in the wall; he also made the four-poster bed. Christa paid $5 per panel for the curtains and dyed the bedspread until she found the color she wanted.

A few steps down to the left of the Keeping Room, a visitor encounters the Tavern Room, formally a large dining room when Billy's parents owned the house. Billy made the fireplace and most of the pieces of furniture. The black chair was one Billy copied from a picture of an early 1600's chair that Christa found in a book. Billy also made the table, where Christa

displays real potatoes, artificial grapes, and a redware ovoid jug.

Christa hollowed out another pumpkin and has filled it with blackberries. She made the sugar cone which sits on a table made by Billy. Christa refers to the red leather chair as 'the find of the century' and for which she paid $5. The small bench in the corner is from The Seraph. The cabinet to its right was rescued from a trash heap. Billy made the cupboard to the left of the fireplace where Christa hangs her smoked hams.

Two early spinning wheels are tucked in the corner.

An elderly friend gave Christa the trunk which had belonged to the friend's father. Although it is of a later period than the décor, Christa would never part with such a sentimental piece.

Dried tobacco leaves hang above the mantel. A tall plum pudding dryer, made by Billy, is displayed to the left of the fireplace. Billy also made all the peels surrounding the fireplace. A taxidermist sold Christa the goose lying on the table.

Christa was able to find most of the clothing, displayed in the bed Billy made, on eBay®.

The black chair at the far end of the table was found for $5.

Billy made the large hutch from old boards given to them by a friend. Christa aged an early tool caddy and tucked it into the opening on the bottom.

The dry sink on the opposite wall was given to Christa by a couple who were entering a nursing home.

Styrofoam mushrooms are laid out on a cutting board on top. Christa buys all her bowls at yard sales, consignment shops, or Goodwill Industries.

Pine boards create a shutter to conceal the sliding door off the back of the house.

Christa purchased the wig on eBay®; it sits on a small antique gate leg table given to her by an elderly friend who wanted Christa to 'give it a good home'. On top, an onion bottle in green was purchased at Hudson's General Store. The corner chair behind it is one of a pair Christa found at the dump when passing by one day. She screamed and insisted Billy turn the car around.

Christa found the bureau behind at a used furniture store; it had thick lacquer and William and Mary drawer pulls before Christa worked her magic.

The large gate leg table in the kitchen is one of the few antiques Billy and Christa own. She admits she paid dearly for it but it is the perfect piece for the area.

The counters are a Formica blend which Billy and Christa purchased at Home Depot. Billy and Christa removed the kitchen cabinets which were painted with thick white paint. Christa saved one, removed the door, distressed it, and uses it now as a display piece.

Christa purchased used burlap on eBay® for $1/yard and created her window treatments.

Christa uses a small room off the kitchen as a buttery. A second sink provides an ideal spot for washing brushes and cleaning up after her crafts. Christa was unable to decide where to plant a cluster of daffodil bulbs; she waited so long that she realized they resembled dried onions. They now hang on the wall with lavender above the sink!

When embarking on a home decoration journey, Christa suggests the first step is to determine what style décor you want to replicate and then use book after book as resources. Christa attributes Joy Henson of Ohio, who was featured in an earlier 'country series' book Welcome Home, and Patricia Ram of Massachusetts, featured in the Joy of Country, as her idols; Christa admits they have been her greatest influence. Emma Sterling, a neighbor and close friend, who will be featured in a future book, has also been an inspiration.

Christa and Billy take pride, and rightfully so, in what they have achieved. They have shown that a creative mind and elbow grease can attain the same results as large sums of money . . . with a greater sense of accomplishment.

Chapter 5

Gaile and Ben Mariano

Gaile and Ben Mariano's 1845 western Pennsylvania farmhouse had remained vacant for many years when they purchased it along with 105 acres in 1995. At the time they lived in a contemporary gated community 15 miles away and weren't ready to take on the massive chore of restoring the home. And who can blame them! Eventually, in 2006, Ben, unbeknownst to Gaile, began working with an architect and contractor to begin the restoration. Unfortunately, the brick had greatly deteriorated and needed to be replaced with siding; however, the beautiful stone foundation was intact.

The front porch was added and the red tin roof replaced. Two years later the house was ready and the transition from suburban living to the country life was underway. That was five years ago and Gaile has since retired as an executive assistant to the CEO of a local hospital and has adapted to country living. Ben's schedule as a radiologist does not allow much time for outdoor chores but Gaile enjoys maintaining the lawn and mowing the fields that are now being leased to a neighbor for organic farming.

The 6000 square foot house is large enough that Ben and Gaile live at one end and occupy primarily the kitchen, large Great Room and adjacent bedroom. The rest of the house consisting of a formal parlor, dining room, five bedrooms and baths is available for visiting family and guests. Despite the size of the house, Gaile and Ben had enough furniture and only supplemented here and there. When they met in 1980, Ben was unfamiliar with antiques and Gaile slowly introduced him to a whole new world. Now they both enjoy antiquing and have specific collections they hunt for, but Gaile admits there is much compromise as Ben enjoys more formal pieces while Gaile prefers country farm tables and stepbacks.

The portrait, an oil on canvas original to New York State, is one of a pair dating to the late 19thC. A rare decorated tanware flower pot sits on the end of the table. In the center of the foyer a hanging four-arm angle lamp dates to the late 18thC.

A collection of early silhouettes hangs over a Chippendale tiger maple slant top desk. A miniature Rayo lamp with its original brass base stands on top.

The formal parlor is painted "El Greco Bronze" by Sherwin Williams. All the mantels are original to the house; this mantel holds two Staffordshire dogs and Limoges plate. Gaile purchased the wall sconces from an auction at the Mountain View Inn, a historical landmark which was being razed.

Across from the desk in the foyer, a one-piece poplar stepback, shown below, with original glass holds a portion of an extensive collection of turkey plates including several pieces of colorful Staffordshire.

Gaile collects dolls from the Annette Himstedt barefoot collection, one of which sits in a bentwood Windsor. The table beside the chair holds a rare Pennsylvania Railroad tea set. The one-piece corner cupboard with original glass holds a collection of Duncan Miller biscuit jars.

Two Windsor side chairs dating to 1820 flank a walnut tavern table. The portrait is the other half of the matched pair.

The corner cupboard, shown below, holds some of Gaile's extensive turkey plate collection.

The dining room is a bit too formal for Gaile's taste and was primarily decorated by Ben. The French clock in the corner was chosen because of its simplicity of design and height. A Greiner straw doll with painted oil cloth face sits near the clock. The contemporary table and chairs were found on a trip to San Francisco.

The picture of the bull is an oil on canvas. A tole painted dough riser sits beneath it on a silverware chest; Gaile waited years for the dough riser and cherishes it.

An alabaster compote holds some of Gaile's stone fruit.

The room across the foyer from the dining room is Ben's toy room. The built-in shelves, once a chimney cupboard, hold a collection of vintage pressed steel Buddy L cars and fire trucks. A very rare elevated railway, one of only eight known to exist, enjoys a prominent place in the room.

A working rare lighted shadow box holds a wood carving of Abraham Lincoln. In front, a two-piece Keystone train sits on the hearth.

The school master's desk, shown below, was found in the basement and is original to the house; it required only minimal restoration to its legs. It holds a glass-encased ship model.

Ben's collection of early doll houses contains, among others, two Moritz Gottschalk pieces seen on the far left of the shelf. A small Noah's ark is the second from the right. The black cleaning lady under the glass dome is an automaton that moves her feather duster when wound, while a vintage Conestoga toy wagon sits in the foreground. A shadow box, front right, shows three Ming figures Ben located on a visit to China. A black chalk figure was found in Tennessee and rests on the window sill.

The mantel holds a carved wooden model of a fox hunt.

A working Calumet clock hangs above an advertising "WATTA POP" dog.

The 7' white farm table with Sheraton turned legs is surrounded with reproduction Windsors.

The walnut pie safe in the corner was found in Indiana. Gaile and Ben liked the unusual drawer and door configuration and its original tins. The picture above was done by Barry Roseland and dates to 1901; it is entitled 'Strawberry Delight' and was found in an old house tucked at the back of a chimney. The log house was done by a local folk artist.

Gaile elected to paint the island red to add a splash of color against her white cabinets. A redware candle can be seen above the sink.

The large eagle was purchased from David Smith from Morrow, Ohio. It was hand-carved by his son, Jason, who created the piece from an original by renowned carver William Schimmel; it is displayed on a Soap Hollow blanket chest. Soap Hollow furniture was produced in the mid-19thC by a select group in Somerset, Pennsylvania.

A collection of stoneware is displayed on top of an early mustard painted cupboard in the hallway. The most treasured of the pieces is the blue and gray water cooler at the far end. A group of skater's lanterns fills the hand-painted shelf found in western Pennsylvania.

The Great Room connects the old farm house with the new addition that is Gaile and Ben's primary living quarters. The two-piece black painted Dutch cupboard retains its original glass and holds Gaile's collection of Flow Blue in a rare Pekin pattern by Wood & Brownfield, circa 1845 England.

A paint decorated red and green jelly cupboard sits in a hallway leading to the master bedroom.

The early walnut grandfather clock is in working condition. The settee was covered by local artist Tom Gillingham using an early coverlet. At the edge of the mantel can be seen two early pewter whale oil lamps.

The rare twelve-light chandelier with embossed brass fonts dates to 1876.

A local artist faux painted the oak pillars. Gaile added old bookcase glass to the transom windows above the French doors leading to the patio.

Two double-arm angle lamps hang in the upstairs landing. A contemporary mirror hangs above a paint-decorated mustard ladies' table. At the end of the landing, a camel back sofa stands behind a painted chest. Another Annette Himstedt doll sits in the Windsor chair beside it.

A miniature yellowware tea set fills a child's pewter cupboard. A sheep pull toy stands on the floor.

The large mustard painted house is actually an architectural model found in West Virginia; the top comes off to display the interior. A sleigh made by folk artist June McKenna stands on top while another Annette Himstedt doll sits in a child's Windsor.

A bedroom in the loft over the kitchen is just large enough for a lovely canopied bed, bureau, and display of early children's toys.

The Moritz Gottschalk dollhouse with a blue roof, dating to circa 1885, was featured on the cover of a book on dollhouses. A nodding donkey stands on the floor and looks out from the railing of the loft into the Great Room toward Nipper, the RCA mascot.

A pair of paper mache figures and a Moritz Gottschalk house stand on top of a mustard painted dry sink.

A bird's eye maple high back bed holds a vintage coverlet and two dolls made by Prickly Pear. The bed is low to the floor so Gaile uses Rockingham bed risers under its legs.

The corner cupboard holds a collection of early quilts. The tilt top candlestand dates to circa 1750 and stands beside an Amish rocker dating to the mid 19thC. The secretary desk is a new piece which Gaile has filled with June McKenna Santa figures. A Rayo lantern sits on the desk. A visitor will always find at least one tree decorated for Christmas somewhere in Gaile and Ben's home.

A small painted chest, perhaps a salesman's sample or child's toy, and a new wig mold stands on a bird's eye maple chest of drawers.

A high post reproduction bed is covered with a contemporary white quilt. Gaile came home one day to find that Ben had placed the painting of Abraham Lincoln over the mantel. She originally didn't care for the look but now enjoys how the picture blends with the blue walls. On either side

hangs a pair of early chipped mirror sconces. The folded flag was one that was flown in Iraq and commemorates her son-in-law's service there.

The beautifully painted four-drawer chest is a Lawrence Crouse piece and is a copy of the original displayed in the Shelburne Museum in Vermont.

A second Crouse painted chest with bun feet can be found in the adjacent bedroom. The twelve-pane cupboard holds a collection of vintage coverlets.

The George Washington andirons date to circa 1810. The mantel holds a collection of tintype framed portraits dating to the 19thC. In the picture above, a child holds a basket of flowers.

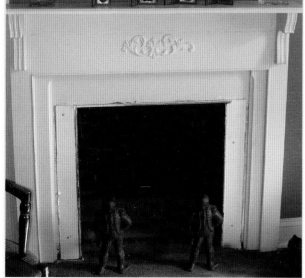

An early painted lady's chair in the corner features a lovely painted design on the back and retains its original rush seat.

A patio garden off the Great Room had recently been planted and overlooks the Laurel Mountains.

Chapter 6

❧ ❀ ❧

Nancy Lindberg and Dan Nelson

Nancy Lindberg has collected antiques for over 30 years. When she and her partner Dan Nelson found their 1850's Norfolk, Massachusetts, home 13 years ago, they didn't think twice. The home was in need of extensive repair, which Dan and Nancy considered an opportunity to begin restoration with a clean palette and to fill the home with early pieces. Dan and Nancy restored the home completely without changing its structural integrity. Dan, who builds motorcycles and rebuilds vintage trucks as a hobby, took naturally to the task of renovating the house. Nancy has been an antique dealer for almost eight years and maintains a shop down the road. As each project was completed, Nancy filled the house with traditional style furnishings she had collected, but then found herself looking for more primitive pieces. In creating a more primitive and earlier period home, Nancy admits that the experience has changed her life; she now grows some of her own produce and buys only organically grown fruits and vegetables. She believes that the change has been healthy and life saving.

Nancy cringes when she notes her maple kitchen cupboards, the next project on her "to do" list. She will either paint or replace them with more primitive-type cupboards that she sells in her shop.

Nancy's floors are a brick-tone ceramic, ideal for upkeep even with a number of pets in the house. Her counters are granite.

Nancy has suspended an early ladder between the cabinets and uses it to display a collection of old egg beaters. Nancy used Benjamin Moore "Cookie Crumb" on the walls throughout most of the house and Old Century "Olde Ivory" for the trim.

Nancy repurposed an early wooden screen to hang over the farm table. The black box was a must have and a piece she says she'll never part with; the open front allows Nancy to display small cutting boards.

Nancy first saw the hutch four years ago, and sometime later it was offered by the owner. She bought it without a re-inspection, and was surprised to find it had been painted white. Nancy spent hours scraping to reveal the natural wood.

Nancy created a cover for an early large wire basket to use as a trash basket.

Many pieces of manganese ware, measures, pantry boxes, and bowls line the shelves. A yellowware milk bowl can be seen on the fourth shelf from the top. Nancy has found that the attic surface pieces and the tones of the unpainted pieces provide a soothing overall effect in a room.

An old apple ladder rests in the corner beside a tobacco, tonic, and cigar sign given to Nancy as a housewarming gift from her mother.

The side entrance off the kitchen is an enclosed porch which Nancy has dressed in a patriotic theme.

The tin bucket is an old *Jiffy Ice Cream* maker which Nancy has filled with red berries. The jelly cupboard was a find for $50! The door in the background, where Nancy has displayed a bunch of Sweet Annie, leans against the original side door to the house. Nancy believes the piece hanging over the jelly cupboard is a float used to spread cement.

The cubby hanging over the gray painted water board holds a collection of favorite tin containers. The cubby was rescued from a chicken coop about to be razed. You might remember in *Just Country Gardens* that the coop is now sitting in the back of Nancy and Dan's house!

An early carrier holds a collection of small earth tone stoneware jugs. The vase holding the feathers is actually a piece of treen displaying lovely lines, I think.

An old doughbox stands in the entrance to the dining room. A hanging shelf with early paint holds a variety of butter presses, molds, treenware, and bowls.

The deep trencher, filled with paddles and rolling pins, was a gift to Nancy from Dan.

Nancy has hung an early yard winder on the wall to the right of the early scrub top round table in the dining room.

A manganese lamp and jug are displayed on top of an early tobacco cutter. Nancy enjoys collecting early pieces with unique shapes . . . hence the appeal of a cog from an old water wheel.

The red hanging cupboard features early chicken wire on the front; Nancy uses it to display her tinware.

Nancy used the original house entrance to create a cozy area filled with primitive vignettes. A carrier with original red dry paint is filled with early paddles.

Ovoid jugs stand beside an early yarn winder perched on a small bench. Beside it on the table rest a small goat's yoke and a small bird's nest filled with abandoned eggs.

An early green painted bench with wonderful form and apron serves as a coffee table; it holds a broom cutter used to cut straw, two iron locks, and a strainer with bird's nest.

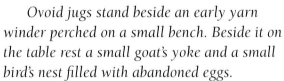

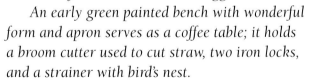

Nancy rescued the delightful rocking horse for $25! What a find! A dough bowl with yarn balls rests beneath it on the small work table.

A Family Heirloom quilt covers the bed in the master bedroom. The table at the foot appealed to Nancy because of its color and cut-out shelf.

A small buggy seat affords height to the bed table which holds three miniature stoneware pieces.

A primitive birdhouse repurposed from a grungy old box stands on top of an oak chest of drawers in the corner.

Dan and Nancy dropped a sink into an early oak sideboard in the downstairs bathroom.

An early chicken carrier fits perfectly under the window and creates a shelf for plants.

A bookcase holds an egg crate on the second shelf from the top that retains some of the original egg shells.

I think Nancy's idea to use a carrier as a towel rack in the second floor bathroom is the kind of decorating hint we can look to follow.

Nancy's shop, Nothings New, is filled with primitives, garden statuaries, and even a tool room for the crafters and collectors of early tools. The shop is located at 224 Dedham Street (Rt. 1A), Norfolk, Massachusetts. Nancy's shop is open Tuesday-Sunday 10-5 and can be reached at 508-384-7666. Nancy can also be found on Facebook by searching Nothings New Norfolk or via her email nothingsnew@verizon.net.

How fortunate that Tracy Dodge owned an Italian Fiat sports car which required constant maintenance and Steve Lipman owned an imported car garage just down the road from Tracy's home in Lewisburg, Pennsylvania. That was 25 years ago! Tracy's father was an auctioneer and antique dealer so her passion for antiques came naturally. Steve quickly developed an interest in antiques and is well versed on the historical pieces they own and sell, as well as, much of the history of the period. In fact, they decided in 1996 to combine their talents and interests into a business and opened a large group shop called *The Yellow Garage* in Mullica Hill, New Jersey.

Tracy and Steve looked at over 100 homes before they found their Piles Grove, New Jersey home 12 years ago. Their realtor happened to be speaking to another realtor who mentioned a house had just come on the market the previous day but had no kitchen cupboards. Steve and Tracy's realtor knew immediately that was the house for them. Tracy and Steve paid full price for the 1989 house, built with old materials, and the almost 17 acres of land. Tracy immediately began staying up till 2:00 AM stenciling and painting each room. Most of the work required cosmetic changes with the exception of one small area off the kitchen which Steve and Tracy converted into a butler's pantry and powder room. They also moved the laundry room to the second floor. All of the Victorian style lighting throughout the house was replaced with pieces by Willard Moses.

Steve and Tracy purchased the carved totem pole twenty years ago at an on sight auction of a retiring antique dealer's home. I loved the detail of the piece and expression!

Steve made the farm table on the front porch with a set of old table legs, stretcher base and board and batten door for a top.

The stain on the house is Olympic 'Russet' and the shutters are painted with Heritage "Barn Red".

The large mortar, shown above, with exquisite form was found at an auction and came from the estate of a pharmacist.

The fish pond existed when Tracy and Steve purchased the house. At the time it was surrounded with large shrubs which their four goats promptly chewed down to the ground. The fence in the background now keeps the goats and four geese out of the pond area.

Steve and Tracy have an herb garden in the back on one side of the built-in swimming pool. Tracy plants a wide variety of herbs and grows Japanese honeysuckle on the fence to attract the hummingbirds.

Upon walking through the front door, you enter a large foyer. Tracy used Old Village "Salem Brick" red paint for the trim throughout most of the house; in the foyer Old Village "Rittenhouse Ivory" is used on the bottom of the chair rail. Steve made the wall box from an old shutter. It conceals the thermostat and is open on the bottom to allow for ventilation. The bench with original red paint is a bed bench found in Maine. Tracy and Steve purchased the large hooked rug dating to the late 1800's from Raccoon Creek Antiques owned by George Allen in Oley, Pennsylvania. The salt-glazed jug, probably an Edmonds of Massachusetts piece, was an eBay® find. A small colorful geometric rug hangs above the wall box.

Tracy painted the mural depicting their property as it looked when they purchased it. The long driveway meanders back and the Christmas tree farm has now been replaced by a hayfield for the goats.

The arm chair is a weaver's chair; higher than a regular chair. It stands beside an early black cupboard. The gathering basket in brown paint is from the Paul Flack collection.

A collection of hooked rugs is displayed in the corner beside one of a pair of pineapple tin sconces dating to the 1920's.

In the opposite corner, a wonderful four color early basket, found in Adamstown, PA is displayed beside a tole painted parade horn. Both pieces stand on top of a small mustard painted cupboard and below a colorful geometric hooked rug.

Tracy's collection of mortar and pestles in original paint fill the mantel which is an early salvage piece. Above the collection hangs a theorem on velvet rendered by GB French, a contemporary Pennsylvania folk artist.

The oval table in front of the couch is an 18thC pine tavern table with stretcher base and purported to have Connecticut origins.

A colorful blue and red striped crib blanket hangs beside the mantel. Naked to the eye are small white dots on the blue background giving it a patriotic theme.

The fan back Windsor chair in the background is a signed Wallace-Nutting piece; an original 1920's reproduction of a Rhode Island Windsor. The rug on the floor is one of many custom-made wool rag rugs Tracy and Steve purchased from one of their dealers in the shop.

The pie safe with original robin's egg blue paint retains the original eight tins. It was found on the eastern shore and dates to circa 1830. On top stands a painted basket and rare brown bottle signed Paul Cushman who is one of the glass makers in Albany, NY. Before the bottle was fired, it appears from the edged marks on the side, the maker used it to play Tic Tac Toe. Beneath the small table in original red paint with taper legs, a dated 1814 ovoid jug can be seen.

A panel and post blanket chest in original red and blue paint dates to 1820 and holds a craftsman sample farm table with drawer. One of the dealers in The Yellow Garage brought it in 16 years ago and Tracy and Steve purchased it immediately. It holds a miniature pitcher, a miniature candlestick and child's platter signed Hack wood – an English maker.

A series of punch hole samplers is displayed beside a corner cupboard with strong soldier blue paint found locally. It dates to the 18thC. The armchair is a barrister's Windsor chair with original grain paint. It is signed by the Boston maker.

The checkerboard table holds a signed handled jug by James Morgan – one of the original stoneware potters. It is a New Jersey piece and is decorated with a wall spring design.

Tracy chose the colors of the study to blend with the magnificent hooked rug. The room is painted with Ralph Lauren "Sand" and Old Village "Salem Brick" red trim. Tracy used Old Village "Cupboard Blue" beneath the chair rail.

A jointed folk art dog, found in New Market, VA stands on top of a lovely slant top country store bin in original blue paint.

A swing handle basket with dark green paint holds dried berries and stands on top of a large corner cupboard with mustard paint and paneled doors. A crib quilt, brought into The Yellow Garage, hangs beside it. The dining room table is an 8' Mennonite meeting house table found in Cape May, New Jersey. It retains its original red paint on the folding legs and a scrub top. A large bowl in original green paint maintains the simplistic look in the room. Eight Windors surround the table; six are contemporary pieces from the 1940's and two are authentic early chairs.

An eight day modern reproduction clock with black and red grain paint stands in the corner. It is a copy of an early Silas Hoadley clock, a clockmaker from Connecticut.

The hanging cupboard with dry salmon paint holds a collection of old redware flasks, banks and pitchers, as well as, miniature stoneware pieces.

The plate rack in original green paint is an American piece and is filled with early slipware. The antique child's high chair says Ezra, the name of Tracy and Steve's grandson.

The early sign over the mantel in the kitchen is one of Tracy and Steve's favorite pieces. It reads Washington Tailor on the front and Washington Cleaners on the back. It was purchased at an auction in Staten Island, New York. The auction had officially ended when one of the staff found the sign covered with

dust in the hayloft. Tracy and Steve were one of only a few people left and were able to purchase it at a very reasonable price.

Tracy uses the mantel to display her vintage folk art farm animals, log cabin and nut-head farmer doll. All of the pieces were carved by a southern New Jersey artist. The fence is German usually found to surround a feather tree.

Tracy has filled the compartment in the English tailor's table with a collection of ironstone bowls. The table has huge fat legs while the top is tiger maple and is ideal for use as an island. The apple green bucket bench is Continental. The apothecary seen in the background holds "everything" according to Steve. Above it hangs an apple green bucket bench filled with redware from New Jersey and Pennsylvania.

Tracy's collection of make-do pin cushions is tucked in the corner on top of a 19thC hanging cupboard with original red paint.

The sink and dishwasher seen on the right of the picture were the only built-ins in the kitchen. The little table beneath the window has an apple green base and on top mustard and red painted stars.

Tracy uses the vintage apple green tin-lidded jars, called Hoosier jars, as her canisters. Early baskets hang above. The cupboard beside the stove, made with old doors, was built by Craig Schneeman whose home is also featured in the book. The cupboard houses the microwave.

The large Lancaster County walnut Dutch cupboard with original red paint was purchased at Country Treasures in Preston, Maryland.

Steve removed the back of an antique carriage box to conceal electrical outlets. A GB French folk art piece hangs above it.

A small room off the kitchen was converted into the butler's pantry and powder room. Tracy painted and glazed the cupboards. The walls were aged with Ralph Lauren Tobacco glaze.

An early child's potty chair in red wash stands beneath a wall decorated with stoneware and yellowware lids. I love the look of this space!

A cupboard found at a salvage yard was built into the powder room to give Tracy space to display her early textiles and vintage child's shoes and clothing.

The framed quilt squares are each signed; one of them by Oscar Wilde. The two portraits are oil on tin. The seaweed mocha bowl is filled with vintage blue rag balls.

The large room off the kitchen at the back of the house is the Family Room. The cupboard on the left in salmon paint conceals the television and was made by a New Hampshire artisan. Beside it stands a stretcher base table with blue paint which Tracy and Steve use as a desk.

A six board chest in blue stands in the center of the upholstered pieces done in the flame stitch pattern.

All of the stoneware jugs and crocks on the gray painted bucket bench are from New Jersey, Pennsylvania or New York. On the second shelf from the bottom, three lidded cake crocks make a prominent statement.

Above the bench hangs a country scene done by contemporary folk artist Bill Rank.

In the back of the room, an oval tavern table holds a peaseware bowl.

The glass front corner cupboard is two pieces and was found in Frederick, Maryland. It has red sponge painted decoration. Tracy and Steve found it and decided to pass on it until they got out to their truck! I guess we know what happened next! The cupboard is filled with spongeware and a few pieces of English Staffordshire in the back.

The large paneled door cupboard with blue paint and red trim was scraped down years ago by a dealer before it was 'the thing to do'. Steve and Tracy couldn't resist it.

A pair of millinery folk art heads rest on top of the 18th country Chippendale chest. The watercolor to the left depicts Martha Washington on horseback.

Tracy and Steve found the queen size bed at a used furniture store and painted it black. The chest at the foot is a six board mule chest in green paint found in Bucks Co. An early wide bodied wooden goose, found at a Virginia auction, lies on top. The rug over the bed is a Shaker confetti rug dating to the turn of the century.

George Washington hangs over the chest shown in the picture above. A firehouse Windsor chair with paint decoration stands beside an 1820's Sheridan chest. An early bowl filled with some of Tracy's collection of sewing notions stands on top.

The large dovetailed pine apothecary dates to the mid 19thC and was found in New Jersey. A client was downsizing and moving into a nursing home and chose to take the apothecary with her. When she got there, she realized it didn't fit, called Steve and Tracy who removed it from the home drawer by drawer and the help of a dolly.

Hogscrapers in paint, as well as, a millinery doll are among treasures displayed on the shelf above.

A smaller apothecary holds miniature peaseware and a scarab which Tracy enjoys collecting.

Craig Schneeman built the vanity and attached tall cupboard in the master bath. Tracy elected to use the bottom of the vanity for towels and baskets. The vessel sink and faucet were purchased at Lowe's.

A simple stencil, 'There's no place like home" surrounds the room.

The upstairs landing sweeps around the large staircase and provides ideal space for pieces even as large as the wardrobe in old black paint. It is constructed with southern yellow pine and was found in Virginia. A New England paint decorated box on top is flanked by two New Jersey stoneware crocks.

In the background, the red wash mule chest belonged to Tracy's family. The matching Windsor stools with blue paint were found at Country Treasures in Preston, Maryland. A large sheet iron running horse weathervane was purchased in Vermont.

The stairwell is lined with early trade signs; a mortar and pestle in gold from a druggist shop; a shoe repair sign from Nantucket; a key representing a locksmith shop, a ceremonial lodge ax and three gold balls from a pawn shop.

The two oil on canvas portraits, of New York origin, were purchased at an estate sale on the north Jersey shore. Two Lawrence Crouse chairs stand on either side of a paint decorated gold and black Pennsylvania blanket chest dating to the early 19thC.

The guestroom was used by the prior owner as a child's room and in repainting it, Tracy and Steven used numerous coats of kilz and paint to cover a Mickey Mouse mural which kept bleeding through. An early hooked rug with heart hangs over the mahogany bed. The coverlets are from Family Heirloom Weavers.

The oyster over red paint jelly cupboard was found in Lancaster County.

A hired man's bed in blue paint fits perfectly under the window.

The bird tree beside the little black corner cupboard was crafted by Daniel Strawser Jr, a Pennsylvania folk artist.

Tracy painted the floor in the laundry room to resemble a floor cloth. The folding screen hides the stackable washer and dryer. The saw buck table in red paint dates to the 18thC and was bought in Delaware.

Tracy framed an early coverlet which hangs above a red painted dry sink filled with sewing necessities.

Rug beaters and a Shaker brush hang on a Shaker peg rack in the corner.

A large collection of Steif bears and stuffed animals line the shelf along one side of the room. The large bear on the floor with the block was a store display window piece and named Isaac by Steve and Tracy's grandson.

This is Tracy and Steve's grandson's room, shown left. The bed is a three-quarter rope bed which has been roped and then covered with a futon making it quite comfortable. The theorem over the bed table is by Bill Rank, a noted Pennsylvania 20thC folk artist who studied under David Ellinger. The Cowden & Wilcox bird jug, seen in the theorem, belonged to the artist and sold at auction for $26,000.

Steve painted the bed in the guestroom matching it perfectly with the Family Heirloom Weave coverlets. A Shaker Tree of Life rug hangs at the head of the bed and two reverse glass checkerboards to the left.

A collection of grotesque face jugs is seen on top of the large jelly cupboard. The jugs were deliberately made grotesque to discourage young people from drinking during Prohibition.

Shorebirds fill the top of an 18thC game hanging rack found in New Jersey. It has carved hex signs and measures a large 6' long.

The single drop leaf farm table with red wash and a single drawer is used as a desk. The rug above it was found in Maryland and has since been seen in an old antique guide. Steve and Tracy aren't sure if it is one of many or the same rug.

Steve's collection of vintage dumb bells, shown above, some painted and some with attic surface fill the dough bowl.

Craig Schneeman used wainscoting in the second upstairs bathroom. I was surprised to see the potted poppy on the shelf; one of hundreds I made and sold at Market Square Trade Show a few years ago.

A collection of early painted gameboards lines the stairway to the bottom floor. A sign on the wall indicates where you're headed!

A small bucket bench holds a variety of both early Indian clubs and juggling clubs. A ship's hull with dry mustard and black paint stands on the shelf above beside an articulated folk art dancing Dan. A standing doughbox with mustard paint holds an early decoy.

The open 18thC pewter cupboard is filled with early stoneware mugs and crocks.

The collection of early 19thC circus figures is called schoenhut. The animals and figures were carved by a German couple who immigrated to Philadelphia. There are also a few 'ramp walkers' amidst the collection which are small figures which when placed on an incline wobble down.

Tracy painted and stenciled the stairs to resemble a stair runner.

The Yellow Garage Shop consists of 6500 square feet of space comprised of 35 dealers. There is a broad scope of antiques and collectibles but many specialize in country furnishings, folk art. The shop is located at 66 S Main Street in Mullica Hill, New Jersey 08062. The shop hours are Wednesday-Sunday, 11am-5pm. The phone number is 856-478-0300. Tracy and Steve maintain a website www.yellowgarageantiques.com. They also are the promoters for the annual 100 dealer show, Festival of Antiques, held the second Saturday in June at the Gloucester Country 4H Fairgrounds.

Chapter 8

⌢ ✿ ⌢

Marian Worley

Marian Worley, who is best known by her nickname Sandy, lives in the original circa 1828 cobbler's shop in Zoar, Ohio. Sandy has maintained an antique shop within her 14 room home and has operated a Bed & Breakfast since 1980. Sandy retired about 11 years ago as a psychiatric social worker and has become active in the Zoar Community Association and village which is rich in history.

Zoar became a community out of economic necessity rather than religious preference in the early 19thC Individual families, primarily comprised of poor peasants and farmers from western Germany were being heavily taxed to pay for Napoleon's War. If families were unable to pay, the male family members were jailed. One woman had a vision in 1817 and led a movement to flee West Germany and travel to London where they enlisted the support of Quakers who provided passage to Philadelphia. Joseph Haga received a land grant and escorted a group to Ohio where the Quakers had purchased 5500 acres of land. The community was named Zoar, taken from the Bible meaning a place of refuge. Since there were more women and children as the men were still imprisoned in Germany, repayment of the loan to the Quakers was near impossible by the individual families. The families decided to form a community thinking that collectively they could earn more money and be able to pay back the loan. At that same time, the Ohio Erie Canal was being built and seven miles was planned to go through the 5500 acres of Zoar land. The government contacted the people of Zoar and provided them with plans to sub-contract the work of digging seven miles of canal. They chose to do the work themselves which not only allowed them to pay the Quaker's the money, but buy equipment and tools and free the imprisoned men in Germany.

The parlor is in the original section of the house built in 1828 as opposed to an addition built 7-8 years later. A lovely walnut gate leg drop leaf table is a focal point in the room. It holds an apple box with smoke decoration filled with assorted stone fruit. The vibrant rug is American made and was purchased locally. A small tea table under the window has beautiful turnings. The corner cupboard which is grain painted is filled with a full service of Gaudy ironstone in the Urn pattern and King's Rose and Queen's Rose china.

A flame mahogany slant front desk fits perfectly between the windows. It is purported to be from Gettysburg. Hanging above it an unsigned oil on canvas portrait looks to be a New York Valley painting. The footstool in front of the wing back chair is an Abercrombie-Fitch leather hippopotamus dating to the 1940's.

At the end of the sofa, a table with butterfly leaves and original blue paint base holds a lamp and 'wild clock'. The clock was made by Roger Wood using an old shoe last. Sandy's daughter and son-in-law thought it was the ideal gift for someone living in the original cobbler's shop.

The large wardrobe at the end of the room is made of poplar with flame grain painted panels. On top, Sandy has displayed some Staffordshire dogs, a bird cage and an early Indian basket.

A large Chippendale mirror dating to the mid 19thC hangs between the windows. The chest below it was found locally by a dealer who told Sandy he had the perfect piece for beneath the window. She agreed! A collection of boxes in early paint is stacked on the floor beside it.

The tilt top table with shoe feet was found at a show in Hudson, Ohio. It is unique in that it has a leg which swings. It is surrounded by four signed painted black with stencil chairs similar to Hitchcock chairs. They were made by William Moore Jr who studied under Hitchcock in the early 19thC.

A large trencher with natural surface and lovely form is smooth to the touch from wear.

The one piece corner cupboard with paneled doors is made of regular and tiger maple.

A huge burl bowl stands on top of the cherry gate leg table. The salmon and blue painted dry sink is from Pennsylvania and is an Amish piece dating to 1898. It is marked LAZ and Sandy has learned that the initials stand for Lizzie Ann Zutsman. When found it was over-painted gray because the salmon and blue were too colorful for an Ohio piece. It was dry scraped down to reveal the magnificent paint beneath. Sandy collects wallboxes and arranges them all in the dining room. Her collection started with the Queen Anne wall box with intricate cutout seen to the left of the glass front cupboard below.

Sandy exhibits many pieces of children's cups and saucers on the shelf in back. One of her prized possessions is the identical pair of painted chalkware deer given center stage on the top shelf.

Look at the size of the burl bowl in the dry sink well!

Two wonderful Windsor chairs flank the large two-piece paint decorated cupboard made by Ralph Brothers of southeast Pennsylvania. Sandy uses the ideal display space to show off her large collection of spatterware.

A wall shelf holds more spatterware and Gaudy Dutch.

Tin and pewter candlesticks surround an Eli Terry 19thC clock with wooden gears which rest on top of a Pennsylvania jelly cupboard with original red paint.

Since Sandy's granddaughter who is now in her early 20's was a little girl, she asked her grandmother if she could have the large Soap Hollow cupboard in Sandy's kitchen. Isn't it spectacular? Sandy purchased it almost 20 years ago before Soap Hollow became a popular collector's item. It has a minor restoration on one leg and is dated 1858.

Sandy uses a peel to display some of her choice cookie cutters. On the wall above it, a small cupboard from Pennsylvania holds early candy and ice cream molds.

A dough bowl on the table holds a grain painted utensil tray filled with butter molds and paddles.

Sandy commissioned an artist in 1978 to create a salt-glazed ornament using one of her Zoar cookie cutters. The creation became an annual tradition and each year a new redware or salt glazed ornament is created and sold by the Zoar Community Association at the Christmas in Zoar festival.

Sandy knew when she saw the exquisite dentil molding on the standing tall clock, now placed in the upstairs landing that, although it was covered with thick paint, there was something good underneath.

They dry scraped it to uncover the original red paint. It dates to circa 1835.

Sandy trained under David Wiggins, an itinerant artist, and stenciled all the walls in this guestroom and other rooms. She cuts her own stencils. The queen size bed is a reproduction. The walnut blanket chest is early and from Pennsylvania. The little wall shelf features Ohio sewer tile animals and redware animals.

The Cobbler Shop Antiques is open Tuesday-Saturday, 11am-5pm. Sandy may be reached at the shop or for reservations at the B & B at 330-874-2600. Her website is www.cobblershop.com

Sandy has 5 rooms available at $125/night. Private baths are available on request. Zoar hosts three annual festival weekends; Christmas in Zoar, the first full weekend in December, Harvest Festival, the first full weekend in August and alternating years Civil War reenactments in September of a garden tour in June. During festival events, Sandy requires a minimum 2 night stay.

Chapter 9

Sue and Joe Frank

Sue and Joe Frank both attended the same grammar school in New Jersey and recently celebrated 48 years of marriage. For 22 years, as they raised their children, they lived in an 1803 brick house full of refinished furniture. After the last child left, they decided to downsize and found an early 1900's house that they were never going to leave. They had a huge estate sale and sold almost every piece of furniture and accessory they owned with the intent of buying only good antiques. Despite the fact that Joe is a busy financial adviser, he enjoys working in the yard and collecting but defers most of the decorating decisions to Sue. After only five years in their downsized home, they took a ride after church and saw a 'For sale' sign on the lawn of a brick 18thC home on historic Old King's Highway. Sue said "Oh", as Joe said "No". For the next few months, they alternated between, "It could be really nice", and "No way!" I suspect by now the reader has surmised that they are now the proud owners of that home. It took Sue a little while to get the house to look as she had envisioned; now, 14 years later, she is completely happy with the outcome.

The Frank's Salem County home is a classic step-down colonial with the main quarters in the larger section and the kitchen and dining areas 'stepped down' from the main structure. Often, the stepped-down portions of the house were added later, as is the case with the Frank's house.

The house was originally the *Seven Stars Tavern* until sometime between 1807 and 1824, when it was purchased by the Quakers. The front door is fully mortised and pegged with raised panels, which are termed "proud", a British term meaning raised higher than the surrounding framework. Notice the small window in the first picture; it was used to serve travelers liquid refreshment from the Cage Bar within the main room—an 18thC version of a drive-up window.

The exterior trim paint is Williamsburg "Governor's Palace Tan". The side door leading to the kitchen is a Dutch door which is split horizontally at the center. The door's low headroom reflects the stature of many of the 18thC occupants.

Joe bulldozed the original asphalt circular driveway and created a clamshell driveway and path typical of many early southern New Jersey colonial homes. Crushed shells were a popular way to surface a wagon's path while enriching the look of the home.

The home's elaborate brickwork was intended to display a mason's expertise. As seen, the house was built in 1762 and the initials "LB" represent the last name of the builder, Lauderback. "PE" stands for Peter and Elizabeth.

Joe created the butterfly garden and enhanced the surrounding garden areas in a style indicative of 18thC gardens. A variety of native plants and shrubs, from holly to rhododendrons, surround the property, while the boxwoods create a symmetrical design.

George Allen, owner of Raccoon Creek Antiques in Oley, Pennsylvania, painted the mural above the mantel. The painting shows Olde King's Highway, which originally ran from Moorestown to Salem in the 18thC. The Seven Stars Tavern sits in the middle of the painting, which also depicts the old courthouse and the church where Sue and Joe were married.

Sue used Historic Philadelphia "Independence Hall Quill" paint in the living and dining rooms.

The walk-in fireplace is typical of taverns and large homes in the mid-18thC; it reflects the influence of early English architecture as noted by the herringbone brick wall.

Joe loves to collect ironware and has gathered an impressive display on the fireplace surround.

A bow back Windsor chair with original salmon paint invites a visitor to sit by the fire.

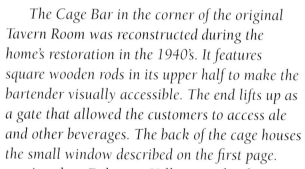

The Cage Bar in the corner of the original Tavern Room was reconstructed during the home's restoration in the 1940's. It features square wooden rods in its upper half to make the bartender visually accessible. The end lifts up as a gate that allowed the customers to access ale and other beverages. The back of the cage houses the small window described on the first page.

A walnut Delaware Valley stretcher base table dating to 1750-1780 can be seen below the hanging pewter cupboard. The William & Mary period table would have been used in the center of a large room; the top is removable for cleaning. The provenance on the table shows it was owned by the Seabrook family of Salem County since the 18thC and passed down to Roger and Doris Seabrook. In the late 1980's, they reduced their antique shop inventory and sold the table to George Allen, who sold it to Sue and Joe.

I gasped when Sue told me she purchased the collection of Peale embossed hollow-cut silhouettes all at one time.

The door leading from the dining room is hung with strap hinges that feature 4' hand-forged iron pins.

Sue purchased the large 19thC glass-front Hackensack cupboard at The Philadelphia Antique Show; she had to sell other antiques to purchase it, much to Joe's dismay. However, Joe has utilized the cupboard to display his collection of early Canton. The platter on top was a gift from Sue to Joe.

The portrait dates to 1825-1830 and is of Delaware Valley origin. The mule chest below, with original red paint, was the first piece Sue purchased from George Allen. One theory as to why mule chests, popular in the 18th and 19thC, were so named is that they could carry as much as a mule. A fan back early Windsor stands on either side.

The tall clock was made by Silas Hoadley; it is dated 1820 and constructed with all wooden gears which require winding every 12 hours. The face is interesting in that it has two dots to replicate key holes but, in fact, it is wound by pulling chains inside the cabinet to raise the weights.

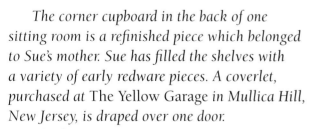

The corner cupboard in the back of one sitting room is a refinished piece which belonged to Sue's mother. Sue has filled the shelves with a variety of early redware pieces. A coverlet, purchased at The Yellow Garage in Mullica Hill, New Jersey, is draped over one door.

The framed wool and linen embroidered square is of southern New Jersey origin; the work, a religiously-inspired piece, is a combination of chain and queen stitching.

The portraits are pastels on paper, circa 1780-1810, depicting two unidentified sitters; possibly they were tavern guests. Based on their naïve and simple dress, Sue surmises they could be Moravian, as an early Moravian Church, dating to 1784, is less than two miles away.

A large-handled basket rests on top of an early four-door cupboard which houses the television. The Chippendale mirror beside it was a housewarming gift from George Allen.

Sue purchased the small six-board chest in front of the sofa from Raccoon Creek Antiques and refuses to sell it back.

The second sitting room off the Tavern Room holds a magnificent corner cupboard with delightful wear and gorgeous blue-green paint. A pair of linen 19thC samplers hangs beside it. The bottom sampler was wrought by an ancestor of one of Sue and Joe's neighbors.

The clock on the mantel is a newer piece—a reproduction of an Eli Terry clock—made by Patrick Terry in 1992. It is flanked by colorful Gaudy Welsh small plates.

Sue favors framed textiles. Hanging over the four-drawer chest with red paint, a framed blue and cream coverlet remnant adds just enough color to the corner in the room.

An array of early baskets, made primarily of oak splint which was popular in the Delaware Valley area, frames the picture of the dining room added circa 1803.

The long narrow sawbuck table was found in Salem County; the X-style leg structure was used in many households both for dining and working. The table's height suggests it was most likely used as a work table. The open country wall shelf in original blue paint with convex scalloped sides dates to the mid 19thC; it was probably a custom-made shelf used to hold small plates, mugs, or other utilitarian pieces. Sue uses the shelf to show off choice pieces of early redware crocks with simple forms and a variety of redware plates. Sue related that during one summer when the interior was being painted, they vacated the house and received a call from the painter. He said he was painting the dining room and did Sue want him "to slap some white paint on the old blue shelf?" Fortunately, he asked!

The hanging cupboard in red paint with nine lights, or panes, dates to the early 1800's; its simple lines and form are indicative of Quaker influence. Sue has placed a number of redware Turk Head molds and small yellowware custard cups for display.

Seen above right, the tall red bucket cupboard is a rare form of Delaware Valley furniture. The paneled doors on the top provide a concealed storage space, but the lower shelf was designed to hold buckets or pails off the floor. Sue uses it to display some of her white-banded yellowware bowls.

The child's chair in the corner was made by Joe's great-great grandfather. Sue and Joe borrowed it when their grandchildren were visiting and no one has ever asked for it back. A framed colorful hooked rug dating to the early 1930's hangs above.

Tracy Dodge and Steve Lipman, owners of The Yellow Garage in Mullica Hill, New Jersey, painted the floor to resemble a floor cloth. Sue uses the 19thC table with splay legs and single drawer as a worktable; the patina of the top is exceptional.

Sue and Joe's home is deed restricted, which means they are prohibited from making any changes to that part of the house built in 1762. The kitchen, however, was added later. When Sue and Joe purchased the house, they removed all the cupboards, refinished them, and redesigned their placement. I love the simplicity of the stoneware crocks lined up on the Corian counter.

Because space in the 18th and 19thC was limited, oftentimes furniture was designed with dual purposes. Such was the case with the chair table, or hutch table as we sometimes call it. The table dates to the last quarter of the 18thC and retains its original red paint. The style of the Windsor bow back chairs dates to colonial times; they were popular because of their comfort and durability. Those that still exist are often painted, as the chairs were often fashioned using different woods and painted to provide a uniform color.

As mentioned earlier, Sue likes to utilize quilt squares and often builds the décor of a room around the colors of the squares. In this guestroom, the green, peach, and cream quilt squares called for a green coverlet at the foot of the bed. The corner cupboard belonged to Sue's mother. The large doll in the chair is Sue's doll from childhood made by her mother. The china doll belonged to Sue's mother.

The bed is Sue's Jenny Lind bed from her childhood.

The guestroom at the back of the house. shown below, was most likely the maid's quarters. The mustard hired man's bed was purchased at The Yellow Garage; Sue and Joe's grandson sleeps in the small bed when visiting.

Sue displays the lithograph of Lincoln which formerly hung in Sue's father's office as a remembrance of her dad; it is dated 1881.

The master bedroom is also done in tones of green with accents from the red and green quilt squares.

The master bathroom features tones of gray with red accents.

Sue chuckled when she cleaned upstairs after a recent guest left; she found two nickels on the sink.

Chapter 10

❖ ✿ ❖

Edna and Bob DeCroo

Edna and Bob DeCroo, both retired teachers, have lived in their western Pennsylvania home for 10 years. Built by Quakers, the home dates to circa 1839, but Bob suspects it is closer to the Civil War period. The previous owners completed most of the restoration, and Edna and Bob added some finishing touches such as replacing some windows and painting.

Bob and Edna are avid collectors and participate in a few shows each year.

The pillar and scroll clock on the mantel in the living room is constructed in the traditional Simon Willard-Eli Terry style; it dates to 1790-1810. Two wooden mechanical locomotives commonly referred to as 'hill climbers' are signed and date to the 1880's. The picture above is a signed hand-painted lithograph by Jennie Brownscombe dated 1910 and is one of two depicting George and Martha Washington that Edna and Bob own.

The long arrow backed settle is circa 1840 and is constructed of poplar and pine; it sits beside an 1810 bow back Windsor. The large corner cupboard is filled with western Pennsylvania stoneware. Bob has enjoyed a fascinating hobby for over 40 years; he researches old towns and old houses and then knocks on doors or gains permission from local authorities to . . . dig. And he finds old artifacts with a 95% success rate. Bob dug up many of the pieces in the cupboard. He pays particular attention to areas where early cisterns may have been located and views such areas as time capsules.

The slant front desk is a true Chippendale New England piece; made of cherry, it dates to the late 18thC. A matched pair of late 19thC Bradley & Hubbard lights retains their original shades. The Chauncey Jerome clock in front of the window dates from the Empire period circa 1840.

The English master ink bottles displayed on the early slant top desk with red paint were ones Bob unearthed. The lithograph above is German and depicts a colorful rendition of children at Christmas.

A stereopticon viewer, popular in the late 1800's as parlor entertainment, is displayed on the end table beside cards depicting worldly scenes.

A triple angle light is attributed to the Pittsburgh area; it was originally a gas light which would have been used in the 1880's and retains its original hummingbird glass shades.

A tiger maple chest can be seen in the back corner; it was found in eastern Pennsylvania and stands beneath an 1840's tiger maple mirror.

The two-piece large walnut cupboard is 1790's and is a western Pennsylvania piece; it holds stoneware jugs, some of which Bob discovered.

In front of the fireplace, a walnut New England Chippendale tilt-top table holds a dough bowl with stone fruit and an early candlestick. Two eastern Pennsylvania chairs with original stencils are part of a set of four dating to the 1830's.

Edna and Bob painted the dining room "El Greco Bronze" by Sherwin-Williams. Edna uses the mantel to display some of her Flow Blue with the Scinde pattern dating to the 1850's. The musket is from western Pennsylvania and is signed by the maker, Andrew Joy. The 9' walnut Sheraton banquet table is surrounded by contemporary chairs by Lawrence Crouse.

The lithograph shows the local area known as Red Lion Valley as it looked in 1880 and includes Bob and Edna's home.

RED LION VALLEY.
1882.

A large turned dough bowl, filled with apples, is flanked by two early brass candlesticks. A clock found in eastern Pennsylvania is a transition Queen Anne-Chippendale and is characteristic of the Rittenhouse Brothers clockmakers. It features a scroll top, fluted corner columns, and a turtle panel at the base. Beside it, an early settle, attributed to the Shaker's, was found in Ohio. The portraits above depict an Indiana, Pennsylvania, couple.

A folk art carved cane stands in a 16-gallon crock, an exact duplicate of one seen in the Westmoreland Museum in Greensburg, Pennsylvania.

An attorney's desk with small cubbies dates to the Civil War and rests between two large stoneware crocks.

Six balloon back chairs, found in eastern Pennsylvania, surround a table located in Lancaster County. The chairs are paint decorated with birds and flowers while the Amish scrub top table has a removable top for cleaning.

Edna collects black folk art from a wide period of time. Many of her pieces have been found locally; a particular favorite is an oil portrait rendered by a local artist from two vintage advertisements.

The twin beds were found at an estate sale in western Pennsylvania and are early Centennial reproductions. Vintage blue and white basket quilts are draped across the foot of each bed. A blanket box with original paint can be seen in front of the window.

The highboy is a Connecticut piece dating to the mid-18thC. Early quilts and vintage coverlets, all from Pennsylvania, are folded on top.

The rocker is a Queen Anne piece dating to the 1770's. Bob made the mirror fashioned after a stylized Chippendale pattern.

The charcoal drawing over the mantel depicts a descendant of Abraham Lincoln and was purchased as part of an estate in western Pennsylvania. The dress comes from the same estate and dates to the Civil War.

A set of early traveling mirrors adorns the mantel.

A late Chippendale mirror, circa 1780, hangs above a Sheraton drop front desk. Pictures of the family from the estate are arranged on the desk.

A turn of the century appliqué quilt dresses the 1810 Sheraton style bed with canopy. The Civil War period armoire in the back corner is called a "breakdown" armoire, as it could be easily dismantled for traveling. Contemporary hat boxes are stacked on top.

The plantation desk with original red wash is a married piece. It is filled with early Lincoln, Civil War, and children's books – many of them first editions. Two handcrafted animals, a deer and horse, were handcrafted from leather and date to the early 1900's.

Cobalt bottles and a master inkwell can be seen on the left side of the desk.

A vintage doll holds a Civil War period parasol on her lap in the corner.

Edna and Bob are particularly drawn, as you might have imagined, to collecting pieces from the Civil War period. They have collected for over 40 years and their Civil War period home has provided the ideal backdrop.

Edna and Bob's property consists of three and a half acres with many garden beds. Edna enjoys gardening and

assumes responsibility for maintaining the beautifully cared for gardens.

The "simply country" book series

by Judy Condon

The Place We Call Home

The Place We Call Home features nine homes showing how homeowners created a home reflective of their ancestry and interests. One Maryland home, two Pennsylvania homes, one Michigan home, one Kentucky home and three Delaware homes are shown.

What's in the "simply country" book series?

Country on a Shoestring
33 tips on how to decorate on a shoestring

Of Hearth and Home
mantels, old painted pieces, signs and primitives

A Simpler Time
log homes, bedrooms, kitchens, dining rooms, folk art and stencils

Country Decorating for All Seasons
holiday doors, porches, mantels, trees, vignettes; summer gardens, and fall decorating

As Time Goes By
The Keeping Room; boxes, baskets and bowls; The Privy; Hallways and Small Ways; The Guest Room

Country at Heart
The Tavern Room; early looms, dolls and bears; The Gathering Room; a kitchen aged to perfection; country gardens

Welcome Home
Over 350 photographs from 2 Connecticut homes and 5 Ohio homes.

Home Again
A house tour book featuring 1 Maine home and 7 Ohio homes including a never before photographed Shaker collection.

The Warmth of Home
3 Massachusetts homes, 1 Pennsylvania home, 3 Ohio homes, 1 New York home and 1 Delaware home

The Country Home
6 Ohio homes, 2 Massachusetts homes, and 1 New Hampshire home

The Comfort of Home
Over 325 color photographs showing a Massachusetts and Ohio home of two exceptional collectors. A Maine home; three Massachusetts homes, one of which is in the city.

Simple Greens – Simply Country
Over 400 color photographs of country homes decorated for the holidays. Also a chapter on "how to make a country bed" and the recipe for the large decorative gingerbread boys and pantry cakes.

The Country Life
The home of antique dealer, Marjorie Staufer of Ohio and Colette Donovan of Massachusetts is featured, as well as 4 other Massachusetts homes, a Maine home, a New Hampshire home and a Connecticut home of children's book author, Mark Kimball Moulton.

Simply Country Gardens
Over 500 color photographs of "just country gardens" from twenty-three homes.

The Spirit of Country
A house tour format book featuring homes in Virginia, Maine, Connecticut, Indiana, Ohio, Massachusetts, New Hampshire and Kentucky.

The Joy of Country
Over 400 pictures of homes in Wisconsin, Upstate New York, Ohio, a Connecticut 18thC home, a doublewide in Delaware, 5 Massachusetts homes, a Pennsylvania home and a Maryland home converted from a 19thC granary.

Holidays at a Country Home
The third holiday book in the series consists of over 500 color photographs of 13 decorated homes and a Condon traditional secret recipe!

A Touch of Country
This book features 8 homes. A unique collection of stoneware and weathervanes is included in one home; primitive settings and collections of early paint are highlights. Rug hookers will love one of the chapters and the avid antique collector will marvel over a Maine home!

Back Home-Simply Country
The renovated 19thC New England cape of Judy and Jeff Condon is featured along with eight other country homes.

Just Country Gardens
Over 550 photographs from 21 different homes. A 'must have' for inspiration and landscape ideas.